NEW VANGUARD • 179

SPECIAL OPERATIONS PATROL VEHICLES

Afghanistan and Iraq

LEIGH NEVILLE   ILLUSTRATED BY RICHARD CHASEMORE

First published in Great Britain in 2011 by Osprey Publishing,
Midland House, West Way, Botley, Oxford, OX2 0PH, UK
44–02 23rd St, Suite 219, Long Island City, NY 11101, USA
E-mail: info@ospreypublishing.com

Osprey Publishing is part of the Osprey Group

A CIP catalog record for this book is available from the British Library.

Print ISBN: 978 1 84908 187 0

PDF e-book ISBN: 978 1 84908 188 7

EPUB e-book ISBN: 978 1 84908 830 5

Page layout by Melissa Orrom Swan, Oxford
Index by Michael Forder
Typeset in Sabon and Myriad Pro
Originated by United Graphic Pte Ltd
Printed in China through Worldprint Ltd

11 12 13 14 15   10 9 8 7 6 5 4 3 2 1

Osprey Publishing is supporting the Woodland Trust, the UK's leading
woodland conservation charity by funding the dedication of trees.

www.ospreypublishing.com

ACKNOWLEDGMENTS

My thanks to "Pockets," Brian, "Fritz," Robert Skipper, Pete G, Rob C, and
Dave for information and imagery. Thanks also to Mathew F Riley, Keith
Widelski, Shaun Tullidge, Tim Linsley, and Kathy and Eddie Schluter for
their continued support.

DEDICATION

Dedicated to my late grandfather WO2 Edward Farrelly, and the men and
women who have served and continue to serve in Operations *Enduring
Freedom* and *Iraqi Freedom* and the International Security Assistance Force
(ISAF). All gave some, some gave all.

AUTHOR'S NOTE

Please note that some unit names and current designations have been
altered or omitted for operational security reasons. Likewise, some
operational details and vehicle specifications and capabilities have
been altered or omitted to safeguard Coalition tactics, techniques, and
procedures. All vehicles, operations, and units mentioned in the text have
been previously made public in open-source reporting.

CONTENTS

SPECIAL OPERATIONS PATROL VEHICLES
AFGHANISTAN AND IRAQ

INTRODUCTION

Special Operations Forces (SOF) have a long history of the use of specialist or customized vehicles adapted to match the unique requirements of their unconventional missions. In the Western Desert during World War II, the Long Range Desert Group (LRDG) used often gaudily camouflaged, and heavily armed, Chevrolet 30cwt trucks alongside machine-gun equipped Willys Jeeps on special reconnaissance (SR) missions. The unit's colleagues in the fledgling Special Air Service (SAS) also pioneered the use of the "Gun Jeep." The SAS mounted daring airfield raids, destroying German aircraft on the ground, and became a major hindrance to Rommel's forces, whilst also proving that raids using specialist armed vehicles were a valid SOF tactic. The LRDG and SAS also developed the concept of what were later termed "mother-ships" – medium to heavy transport trucks driven far behind enemy lines to act as mobile resupply points, allowing the SOF to undertake longer patrols without recourse to traditional resupply channels.

Later in the war, in Europe, the SAS continued with the successful employment of armed Jeeps, adding further field modifications that included crude ballistic glass and light armor, effectively producing a very early precursor to today's heavily armored High-Mobility Multi-Purpose Wheeled Vehicle

An Australian SASR LRPV deployed in Iraq in 2003. This vehicle's four-man crew is typically well armed, with the main .50 M2, forward-mounted FN MAG 58, Javelin ATGM (just visible in its casing to the left of the rear crew member), and camouflage-painted 7.62x51mm SR-25 sniper rifle strapped to the hood in front of the driver. What appears to be a sniper's drag bag is seen just ahead of the SR-25 and may contain a second sniper rifle, possibly a .50 AW-50 or Barrett. (Courtesy ADF SOCOMD)

(HMMWVs; "Humvees"). The US Army made extensive use of both armed and armored Jeeps for reconnaissance duties by conventional forces and by the Rangers in the European theater (the Rangers also utilized so-called "Machine-Gun Jeeps" in combat patrols during the Korean War).

Postwar, SAS operations in Oman saw the revival of the concept in the form of a number of Series One Land Rovers modified to mount twin Vickers medium machine-guns (MMGs) and a pair of Browning .30 MMGs for deployment on recce missions. (Note that "recce" is the abbreviation for "reconnaissance" used in both British and American Tier One SOF terminology, as opposed to the more common American or Australian "recon.") The legendary SAS "Pink Panther" – a heavily customized Land Rover 109 that gained its nickname from the pink tone initially used as remarkably effective camouflage paint – was first deployed in the late 1960s during the SAS's counterinsurgency operations in Aden. The 109 allowed longer-range operations due to its increased payload capacity and additional fuel tanks, and was more heavily armed through the integration of the big Browning M2 .50 heavy machine-gun (HMG). The Pink Panthers became as much an icon of the SAS as Jeeps were during the campaigns in the Western Desert. They continued to serve with distinction until the late 1980s, when they were replaced by new model SAS "Landies" – the Land Rover 110 Desert Patrol Vehicle (DPV). However, even with the adoption of the new model DPV, the nickname "Pinkie" stuck.

The US and Australian militaries were also developing similar platforms for their SOF during the 1960s and 1970s. The US Army Rangers famously used their M151 Gun Jeeps with mounted single or twin M60 General Purpose Machine-Guns (GPMGs), as did infantry and mechanized scout platoons in Vietnam, where the vehicles often served as convoy escorts for supply columns, speeding to position and suppressing ambushes. The Ranger Gun Jeeps were later to deploy to Grenada during Operation *Urgent Fury* in 1983 and subsequently to Panama during Operation *Just Cause* in 1989.

The Australians followed the UK Special Forces (UKSF) example for their Special Air Service Regiment (SASR), and modified Land Rover Series 2As as the Long Range Patrol Vehicle (LRPV), before eventually adopting the now famous six-wheeled Jaguar Perentie LRPV. The SASR had the unenviable task of conducting long-range reconnaissance and surveillance operations in Australia's barren far north and their vehicles were suitably enhanced for the grueling conditions. Such experience, and that of 22 SAS in Oman and Aden, would still be extremely pertinent decades later in Iraq and Afghanistan.

The next major evolution in SOF vehicle-mounted operations occurred during the 1991 Operation *Desert Storm* to liberate Kuwait after Iraqi forces invaded the tiny, oil-rich nation. US and UK SOF deployed in the infamous "Scud Hunt" for Iraqi Scud ballistic missile platforms, aiming to inhibit Iraq's capability to launch missiles into Saudi Arabia, Israel, and Bahrain. Both 1st Special Forces Operational Detachment – Delta (SFOD-D or Delta) and Operational Detachment Alpha (ODA) teams from the 5th Special Forces Group (Airborne) conducted long-range SR mounted and foot patrols to uncover the Scud

An exceedingly rare image of the original DMV HMMWVs in use by Delta in the 1991 Gulf War. Despite its poor resolution, the image shows the extensively modified early M998 and M1026 versions. Of particular interest is the apparent lack of heavy crew-served weapons mounted on the two vehicles in the foreground, with M249s and M60s apparently the extent of their armament. The rear vehicle appears to mount an M2 .50 in some form of ring mount, but the image is not clear enough to identify the vehicle – it may well be a Land Rover variant. (Courtesy USSOCOM)

The famed US Navy SEAL DPV shown deployed in southern Iraq. Both weapons visible on this three-man version are covered to protect against the sand. (Courtesy US Navy, photo by Photographer's Mate 1st Class Arlo Abrahamson)

launchers and call in Coalition airstrikes. Some of these operations utilized so-called Special Forces Desert Mobility Vehicles (DMVs), early variants of which would later become known as Ground Mobility Vehicles (GMVs). These were standard M998 and M1026 HMMWVs enhanced with integrated specialist communications, improved suspension, and increased cargo capacity and weapons stations (apparently some Land Rover-based vehicles were also modified and used by Delta during the campaign). The UKSF contribution from 22 SAS included recently acquired 110 DPVs, supported by Unimog and ACMAT trucks acting as mother-ships, in turn protected by a number of modified Defender 90 Land Rovers.

In addition, the Gulf War saw the operational debut of a new concept in SOF vehicles known variously as the Light Strike Vehicle (LSV) in UKSF service or as the Desert Patrol Vehicle (DPV) in US Navy service. Essentially an upgraded, armed, two- or three-seat dune buggy, the LSV was operationally trialed by 22 SAS in Iraq's western deserts, found wanting, and quickly retired, although the US Navy SEALs (Sea, Air and Land teams) adopted the DPV and

A **LAND ROVER 110 "PINK PANTHER" DESERT PATROL VEHICLE (DPV): MOBILITY TROOP, D SQUADRON, 22 SPECIAL AIR SERVICE REGIMENT (22 SAS), IRAQ, 2003**

Potentially the most famous Special Forces vehicle of all time, the SAS Pink Panther, or "Pinkie," is evocative of the Regiment's origins in North Africa in World War II with David Stirling's fledgling Special Air Service and its compatriots in the Long Range Desert Group (LRDG). In a number of ever-improved variants, the Pinkie saw action in 22 SAS for nearly 40 years, to be finally replaced by the Supacat Menacity in 2003–04.

The example illustrated shows the last model developed and deployed by 22 SAS for the invasion of Iraq in 2003, when B and D Squadrons operated together as Task Force 7 in western Iraq. This Pinkie is fully "tooled up" with a .50 Browning and passenger-side General Purpose Machine-Gun (GPMG) and carries an impressive amount of supplies, indicating its probable role in long-range reconnaissance.

Note the heavily chipped finish of this vehicle, indicating heavy use – it may well be one of the Pinkies that took part in the earlier Operation *Trent* in Afghanistan – and the sand channels for recovering the Pinkie from bogging in soft sand. The three-man 22 SAS crew are all wearing a mix of commercial and issue equipment.

were famously photographed as they drove several of the vehicles into Kuwait City at the conclusion of the ground campaign.

Between 1991 and 2001 there were relatively few instances of SOF-specific vehicles being deployed in action. The Rangers and Delta operators of Task Force Ranger in Somalia in 1993 used standard HMMWVs during the infamous Battle of the Black Sea, although reports indicate there was also at least one SEAL DPV present. Several DMV variants were deployed, however, with US Army Special Forces ODAs in other regions of the war-torn country.

Operations in support of the Implementation Force (IFOR) and later Stabilization Force (SFOR) in the Balkans also saw a mix of regular HMMWVs and DMVs deployed with Army Special Forces. Meanwhile, on the other side of the world, the UK's 22 SAS and Special Boat Service (SBS) deployed several Pink Panther DPVs (including one mounting an unusual twin M2 .50 weapons station) immediately prior to Operation *Barras*, the successful hostage rescue in volatile Sierra Leone conducted after a number of British servicemen were taken prisoner by local militia.

After the fateful events of September 11, 2001, the ensuing Operation *Enduring Freedom* in Afghanistan (OEF), and the later Operation *Iraqi Freedom* (OIF), have shared extensive and on-going use of SOF, which truly became the "tip of the spear." OEF began with the October 2001 SOF- and CIA-led campaign that toppled the Taliban government and inflicted heavy losses on Osama bin Laden's al-Qaeda terrorist organization, which had taken up residence in the country at the invitation of the Taliban leadership under the movement's founder, Mullah Omar.

A similarly heavy reliance on SOF was later evident in Iraq during OIF, with SOF seizing key targets and acting as the eyes and ears and as a flanking screen in the western desert for conventional forces driving from the south toward the capital. Additionally, SOF in the form of the 3rd and 10th Special Forces Groups led operations in the north when Turkey withdrew over-flight permissions for US forces. Following the April 2003 invasion, SOF have continued to operate extensively in support of the Coalition's counterinsurgency effort throughout the country, constantly adapting and modifying their tactics and techniques against an elusive insurgent opposition whose key weapon has become the roadside bomb or improvised explosive device (IED).

SOF vehicles have also evolved to meet the mission requirements of, and the divergent threats posed by operations in both Iraq and Afghanistan. The question of armor and survivability versus speed and maneuver has become one of the most public aspects of this evolution, typified by recent media interest in the use of the IED-vulnerable Snatch, Snatch 2, and Weapons Mount Installation Kit (WMIK) Land Rover platforms by UK forces in both theaters. SOF vehicles must be suited to operating in rough or mountainous terrain yet also pack enough punch so that they can extricate themselves if engaged by a numerically superior enemy.

Mounting weapons capable of engaging enemy armor is less of an issue. With the exception of the relatively short invasion phase of OIF, and the occasional Taliban-controlled armored vehicle still operable in late 2001, the threat of enemy armor in both theaters is nigh on zero, and Javelin and similar manportable systems are carried to engage any enemy vehicles, such as the ubiquitous "technical" or armed pick-up truck, which are encountered. SOF vehicles consequently must be able either to outrun or outgun potential adversaries based on the risks envisioned within the theater of operations. They must also be able to act as mobile logistical bases, transporting enough supplies for the SOF operators to replenish in the field without recourse to frequent, and potentially compromising, helicopter resupply. The necessary trade-offs between speed, maneuverability, and protection – in terms of armor, in-built survivability systems such as fire suppressors and blast deflectors, and weapons systems – must also be considered, particularly in light of the increased threats from Soviet-era "legacy" mines in Afghanistan and IEDs of some 90 different types in both theaters.

OPERATION *ENDURING FREEDOM*

An Overview

The inhospitable mountains, harsh desert plains, and fertile river valleys pose almost unique challenges for SOF ground mobility in Afghanistan. Depending on their role and specific operational needs, SOF may be required to operate their vehicles in a mixture of these terrain types, with each offering its own particular hazards for wheeled and tracked vehicles. For example, the so-called "Green Zones" along the river tributaries and irrigation networks ideally require smaller, lighter, more compact vehicles to negotiate the often narrow roads and trails, and to limit the chances of becoming stuck in bogs. Conversely these Green Zones are ideal locations for ambush by opponents using heavy, crew-served weapons and/or IEDs because of the natural cover and concealment. This threat of ambush may necessitate the use of more heavily armored vehicles, such as the tracked Viking used by the UK Helmand Battlegroup or the Strykers deployed by the US Army Stryker Brigades and Rangers. Likewise in the mountains of eastern and northern Afghanistan, vehicles such as the Tacoma or Hilux commercial pick-up truck successfully navigate the often treacherous trails far more easily than a wider-wheelbase vehicle such as the HMMWV. Yet it goes without saying that these civilian-designed trucks do not have the payload, armour, communications, or weapons systems of a HMMWV, Supacat, or similar dedicated platform, and compromise becomes all too necessary.

Patrol vehicles used by the opposition. A captured Soviet-produced UAZ-469 used by the Taliban, with what appears to be a BM-12 rocket pod mounted on the rear. The white paint over the home-sprayed camouflage pattern may be a reference to the Taliban flag or simply a crude IFF marker. (Courtesy JZW)

Along with these natural environmental challenges, there are the man-made dangers from both legacy mines – in anti-tank and anti-personnel variants – and the IEDs of the Taliban insurgents and al-Qaeda. Estimates of the number of mines deployed by Soviet forces in their decade-long war with the *mujahideen* and the subsequent Afghan Civil War range from 250,000 to 400,000, according to the Halo Trust de-mining charity. Some of these Soviet minefields were correctly recorded on maps or later made safe by Soviet combat engineers, but many were not.

A early SF HMMWV, resplendent in unusual field-applied camouflage, used by the 19th Special Forces Group in Afghanistan, 2002. Just visible inside the open forward compartment is a Blue Force Tracker, and a SATCOM antennae array has been deployed in the rear storage area. (Courtesy JZW)

In addition, thousands of mines were air-deployed from Mil Mi-8 helicopters and never marked, although the majority of these were anti-personnel types such as the notorious PFM-1 "butterfly mine," and thus pose a much greater threat to Coalition foot patrols and civilians than vehicles. Even after the Soviet–Afghan War and Afghan Civil War between the Democratic Republic of Afghanistan (DRA) government and the *mujahideen*, mines continued to be laid by both the Taliban and the Northern Alliance in their close to ten-year struggle for control of the country.

Mines have also helped to feed the major IED threat to Coalition vehicles in Afghanistan. Although much of the explosive content of IEDs comes from unexploded or looted artillery and mortar rounds, along with traditional ammonium nitrate-based fertilizer, mines are also recovered by the Taliban insurgents, who extract the explosives to be used in IEDs. Often several mines will be "daisy-chained" together and detonated by command wire or pressure plate.

During the initial years of OEF, the sophistication of IEDs in Afghanistan was generally low in comparison to those used in the burgeoning insurgency in Iraq, whose bombmakers were often advised by former Iraqi Army personnel and seasoned jihadists from the killing fields of Chechnya and Lebanon. Most devices were reasonably simple command wire, timer, or pressure plate triggered devices with a relative scarcity of secondary devices or tamper switches. The advantage of their simplicity was their ease of construction, and thus they could be manufactured and deployed in large numbers (it should be no surprise that the IED factories are prime targets of SOF operations; the safest way to defeat the IED is at its source).

Since around 2005, however, there has been a marked increase in the sophistication of Taliban IEDs. Explosive Ordnance Disposal (EOD) and Weapons Intelligence officers report the use of tamper switches (which effectively operate as a back-up initiator that cuts in if EOD officers disrupt the primary detonator), and the gradual but wider application of the infamous Explosively Formed Penetrator (EFP), which offers far greater potential penetration of armored vehicles through its use of a crude but frighteningly effective shaped-charge penetrator. EFPs also provide a stand-off capability, with the device triggered by infrared (IR) beams – often these triggers are nothing more innocuous than commercial passive infrared sensors of the type found, for example, in home security devices or even television remote controls. It is suspected that this knowledge has been provided by members of the Iraqi insurgency, covert Iranian Pasdaran (Revolutionary Guard) elements, and international Salafist jihadists.

The campaign against the IED in Afghanistan is intrinsically different to the situation in Iraq where, mirroring the British experience in Northern Ireland, many large IEDs are planted in roadside culverts – the amount of tarmac road in much of Iraq makes digging a hole for, planting, and concealing an IED that much more difficult. Afghanistan is primarily a land of unimproved dirt roads and tracks; it has few culverts, which in Iraq have been sealed or monitored with much success.

Whether operating as part of the NATO International Security Assistance Force (ISAF) or within the American-led OEF, SOF tactical use of vehicles primarily falls into two broad mission types – SR (or recce) and direct action (DA). Vehicle-mounted SR ranges from "presence" patrols aimed at reassuring the local civilian populace and deterring Taliban activity, to long-range covert patrols to identify high-value targets or key enemy nodes, such as command-and-control cells, bombmakers, or logistics networks. Often an SR operation may result in either an airstrike by Coalition fast air on the identified target or, in limited cases, a heliborne direct action against the target by other SOF.

An example of a vehicle-mounted SR operation leading to a DA is that conducted by C Squadron, SBS, to kill Mullah Dadullah, a Taliban senior commander, southeast of Kandahar in May 2007. After tracking the target with the assistance of the US Joint Special Operations Command (JSOC) surveillance unit, "Gray Fox," an SBS troop-strength patrol in Supacat 4x4 High Mobility Transporter (HMT) 400 and 6x6 HMT 600 patrol vehicles, along with trail bikes for route reconnaissance, carried out a covert reconnaissance operation. Infiltrating at night to within visual range of Dadullah's compound, the SBS reported that an airstrike might not necessarily ensure the death of the designated high-value target (HVT). Instead, a night-time heliborne assault by the rest of C Squadron was launched, killing more than 20 defenders and resulting in the death of Mullah Dadullah.

Similar operations carried out by the Australian SASR have resulted in the deaths or capture of numerous high- and medium-value targets in Uruzgan Province, with the SASR soldiers effectively stalking their targets in their LRPVs until the opportunity presents itself to direct in Coalition air assets to engage the target decisively. A patrol vehicle can then be driven into the target area if necessary, under the protective over-watch of sister callsigns (other elements of the patrol covering the team), to conduct a Bomb or Battle Damage Assessment (BDA) and collect forensic evidence and/or retrieve DNA samples for confirmation of the target's identity.

An early US Army Special Forces HMMWV in Afghanistan mounting a most unusual weapon system, the Soviet DShK 12.7mm HMG complete with IR spotlight. The vehicle may have been deployed with the fledgling Afghan National Army SOF. (Courtesy ABNINF)

The vehicular nature of these patrols means they can stay in the field for far longer than a foot patrol inserted by helicopter or parachute, and allows relatively easy extraction if significant opposition is encountered. Vehicles are also often utilized in support of Sensitive Site Exploitations (SSE), which involve a systematic search of a target location that has already been engaged by air power or other ground forces. An example was the SSE conducted at the massive cave complex located at Zhawar Kili, where SEALs from Team Three inserted several DPV dune buggies by sling load under US Army Chinooks to act as a mobile blocking and reaction force.

DA operations are, as the name suggests, rather more offensive in nature than reconnaissance missions. In these SOF will infiltrate a target area to seize an objective, raid a location, engage a known enemy cell, or to capture or kill an HVT individual. DA operations will generally be conducted at night to maximize the advantages of the Coalition's advanced night-vision and thermal-imaging systems, and will be between troop (16 men) and platoon or even squadron strength (30–70 men) to ensure the necessary amount of firepower can be brought to bear if required.

Often Afghan forces, either Afghan National Police (ANP), Afghan National Army (ANA) or even locally recruited Afghan militia forces (AMF), will accompany the SOF DA units in their Toyota 4x4s or HMMWVs to "put an Afghan face on the operation". Many raids or "snatches" have been conducted by SOF in concert with these local forces, as the indigenous troops bridge the language gap and can often pick up on barely perceptible signs that a suspect individual is a Taliban, along with providing useful extra "muscle."

Another variant of the DA mission is SOF serving as a vehicle-mounted quick reaction force (QRF), a role often undertaken by the Rangers in the early period of OEF as they protected the forward-deployed safe houses from which the CIA, Delta, and ODA members operated. SOF may also be tasked to operate *in extremis* as a vehicle-mounted Combat Search and Rescue (CSAR) element to rescue downed aircrew, such as in the first few weeks of the Afghan campaign, when flying in dedicated CSAR helicopters from Pakistan or Uzbekistan proved problematic both politically and geographically.

A close up of a Toyota Tacoma deployed by an ODA in Afghanistan and featuring an M240 mount attached to the rollbar and field expedient racks carrying fuel and ammunition. (Courtesy JZW)

Non-Standard Tactical Vehicles

In the landlocked country of Afghanistan, the initial SOF teams were inserted by helicopter, often under extremely testing weather and geographical conditions. During these early days, the men of the Army ODAs, CIA "Jawbreaker" teams, JSOC, and UKSF were forced by the logistics of inserting vehicles by helicopter into such an inhospitable region to rely on locally procured vehicles sourced through Northern Alliance "fixers," until military vehicles could be flown in later in the campaign (Delta was one exception which managed to air-drop a number of its Pinzgauer 6x6 patrol vehicles into the country in October 2001). The famous images of ODAs in their Toyota Tacoma and Hilux pick-up trucks quickly became as synonymous with the Afghan campaign as images of the Special Forces' use of Afghan ponies as alternative "local" transport.

The use of civilian vehicles was so widespread that a new term entered the SOF lexicon: the Non-Standard Tactical Vehicle (variously the NSTV or simply NTV). The use of such vehicles was deemed acceptable because they allowed the SOF to maintain a low profile in-country and it was relatively easily to procure replacement parts through Afghan channels. The fact that the four-wheel drive vehicles were ideally suited to the tough geographic environment was amply proven by their use by both the Northern Alliance and their opponents in the Taliban and al-Qaeda. The Taliban, in fact, used pick-up trucks both as a form of mobile gun platform, with crew-served weapons bolted down in the cargo bed, and as an *ad hoc* personnel carrier.

The NSTVs were initially simple commercial Toyota Hilux trucks in both single- and dual-cab models with minor field-expedient customizations added by the ODAs themselves, including jury-rigged machine-gun mounts and cargo boxes. The British initially arrived with a number of white-painted Land Rover Defenders that had been fitted with a roof-mounted GPMG – famously seen at the siege at the Fort of War at Qala-i-Janghi – and a number of Toyota Land Cruisers. A small number of lightly armored Mercedes G-Wagens were donated by Norway and also pressed into service by US SOF. On at least one memorable operation, Delta approached an al-Qaeda target

A fascinating shot of a US Army CH-47 Chinook in Afghanistan about to lift off with an early-model SOF GMV in a sling load. A Polaris ATV sits nearby. (Courtesy JZW)

SPECIAL FORCES ENHANCED CAPACITY VEHICLE (ECV): OPERATIONAL DETACHMENT ALPHA, 5TH SPECIAL FORCES GROUP, IRAQ, 2008

This cutaway illustrates a recent ECV built from an M1113 body. Clearly illustrated are the open heavy-weight armored doors fitted as crew protection against the ubiquitous roadside bombs, along with an up-armor package applied directly to the chassis. The amount of armor clearly delineates this ECV as one routinely used for urban missions, known in military parlance as Military Operations in Urban Terrain (MOUT) where the threat of IEDs and RPGs is perhaps highest. In rural operations, the Special Forces generally use the more lightly armoured GMV-S with the open tray back alongside commercial SUVs.

The turret features an Objective Gunner Protection Kit (O-GPK) with transparent windows to increase the gunner's situational awareness. The O-GPK features the fearsome M134 7.62x51mm minigun, more generally found mounted in helicopter door-gunner positions, but sometimes used on the lead vehicle in SF mounted patrols in urban environments due to the amount of suppressive fire the weapon system is capable of. Other ECVs and/or GMV-Ss in the patrol would carry a more typical mix of M2s and Mk47s along with M240s and Mk48s fitted as secondary weapons in MSG mounts.

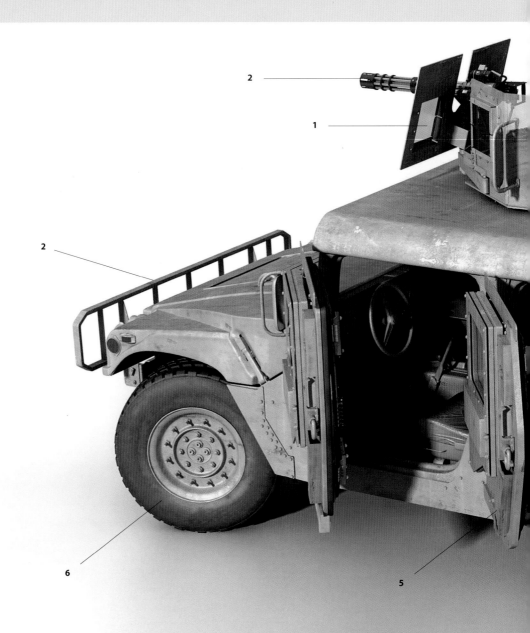

3

4

compound concealed in local "jingle trucks" – the commercial trucks often fitted with a bewildering array of trinkets, and painted in garish colors, used by Afghans to transport all manner of goods.

Later, Toyota Tacomas, the US domestic version of the Hilux, were purchased in the United States, modified at Fort Campbell, and flown into Bagram. These Tacomas were typically the four-door dual-cab models and were equipped with supercharged engines and other modifications, which included: IR filters on the headlights; military vehicle antennae to facilitate VHF, UHF, and satellite communications; the addition of Blue Force Tracker units; and a rollbar-fitted weapons mount (generally mounting the M240B machine-gun, although some examples featured the M249 Squad Automatic Weapon – SAW – and in at least one case the Russian-made PKM machine-gun). In 2002, US Special Operations Command (USSOCOM) even sourced an armored version of the NSTV known as the Hardened Sports Utility Vehicle (HSUV), which had bodywork designed to withstand small-arms fire and offer some limited protection against IEDs.

Ground Mobility Vehicles

As the SOF presence grew in November and December of 2001, specialized military light vehicles arrived with the SOF. Chief amongst these were the Ground Mobility Vehicles (GMVs) of the US Army Special Forces. GMVs were developed following trials conducted after 1985 by USSOCOM on modified HMMWV platforms for SOF use, known then as the Desert Mobility Vehicle System (DMVS). The DMVS program had resulted in the DMVs used by the 5th Special Forces Group and Delta "Scud Hunters" during Operation *Desert Storm*.

The GMV itself is the next generation of the venerable DMV, again incorporating hard-learnt lessons from the 1991 conflict. Based on the M998 or M1025 HMMWV, the GMV features: a new suspension system, increasing the payload capacity to 2½ tons; extra fuel tanks that triple the vehicle's range; added bustle racks for ammunition, fuel, and water; an internal fire suppression system; multiple smoke-grenade launchers; a turbocharged diesel engine; wiring for permanent satellite communications; a new radiator designed specifically for desert operations; IR headlights;

SEAL Team 10 GMV-N on operations with the NZ SAS in Afghanistan, 2005. Note recovery tools strapped to the hood and the excellent view of the swing-arm mounted 7.62x51mm Mk 48 Mod 0 GPMG, a hybrid of the M240 and the M249, specifically developed for USSOCOM. The main weapon system is the Mk 47 Striker 40mm AGL, the US version of the Heckler & Koch GMG used by UKSF. (Author's photo)

and the capability to charge batteries for communications sets and thermal sights (and, as one ODA member wryly commented, coffee makers) via a DC/AC converter.

In terms of weaponry, the GMVs feature a swing-arm weapon mount on the passenger side doorframe able to take an M240 or M249, whilst later versions often have a second swing-arm mount in the rear bed supporting either a second M240 or M249 or the newer SOF-developed Mk 48 MMG. The GMV has a standard roof ring mount and in the early days of Afghanistan were universally equipped with the M2 .50 HMG or the Mk 19 40mm automatic grenade launcher (AGL). Some later versions of the GMV offered the capability to mount a secondary weapon on the roof weapons station, most often an M249 SAW or Mk 46 machine-gun, for use when the principal weapon (the Mk 19 for instance) was not suitable for either tactical or collateral-damage reasons.

A US Army Rangers GMV-R mounting a 40mm Mk 19 pictured during exercises before deployment to Iraq in 2005. Of interest is the Para SAW mounted on the swing-arm bracket behind the driver. (Courtesy US Army)

The GMVs deployed in support of the ODAs in late 2001 featured no armor packages, although some teams eventually received limited examples of the M1114 "up-armored" HMMWV variant in early 2002. In fact, during the 2002–03 periods, an ODA would typically travel in one GMV, an M1114, and a pair of Tacoma or Hilux trucks (which were often relied upon particularly in the north, where the roads were not wide enough for the GMVs and HMMWVs). Special Forces at this time preferred the speed and relative agility of the un-armoured GMV, which was often stripped of doors and even the windscreen both to reduce weight and to allow the crew to fire unimpeded out of the vehicle with their personal small arms. As the scourge of IEDs began to increase in-theater, however, the SOF attitude toward armor changed, and with it the basic GMV design evolved to attempt to meet the threat.

Army Special Forces were not the only SOF units using the GMV in Afghanistan. The Canadian Joint Task Force-2 (JTF-2), often referred to as the Canadian equivalent of Delta or 22 SAS, also drove a GMV version, as did the New Zealand Special Air Service Group (NZ SAS) in its early deployments (borrowed from the resident US Special Forces Groups).

When first deployed, the Navy SEALs also used a mix of early GMVs and regular HMMWVs; as in Somalia, these vehicles were again donated by the US Army, but in this case by the Rangers who were forward-deployed for OEF in Oman. The SEALs complained about the state of the vehicles that were made available to them, these often being the "clapped-out" left-over vehicles that the Army no longer required. Whether this was a result of inter-service rivalries or simply the natural result of the over-extended supply lines is unclear. The SEALs ensured that the GMV-N (Navy) variant was soon moving into production and that each operator deploying received specialist mobility training. Surprisingly, a similar situation later occurred in Iraq in 2003, when SEALs in post-invasion Baghdad were again forced to use US Army cast-offs, in this case the M1035 soft-top ambulance model, until they managed to source loans of Spanish up-armored HMMWV copies and eventually their own up-armored GMV-Ns.

Quads and Bikes

Besides the GMV and the NSTV, potentially the most useful vehicle deployed by US SOF is the All Terrain Vehicle (ATV), also known as a Quad Bike. ODAs are generally supplied two per ODA team. These 4x4 and 6x6 platforms are utilized for replenishment and resupply, casualty evacuation, and even advances to contact. The ATV of choice in the early days of the Afghan deployment was the Polaris MV700 4x4 with both factory and in-theater modifications, although the diesel-powered John Deere M-Gator was also deployed, mainly as a logistics carrier within the confines of Patrol Bases (PBs) and Forward Operating Bases (FOBs). The M-Gator proved popular, as the off-the-shelf 6x6 vehicle can carry upwards of 600kg (1,320lb) of equipment and can be transported in both the MH-53 and MH-47 helicopter.

Modifications to the Polaris included run-flat tires, ancillary fuel tanks, bustle racks for water and ammunition, and mounting brackets for M4 carbines. Delta also deployed with a custom version in 2001 that featured exhaust silencers and IR headlights. Many of these modifications were later

---

C

1: PINZGAUER SPECIAL OPERATIONS VEHICLE (SOV): NEW ZEALAND SPECIAL AIR SERVICE GROUP (NZ SAS), AFGHANISTAN, 2005

Deployed by both the NZ SAS in Afghanistan and US Army Delta in Afghanistan and Iraq, this SOV variant of the Model 718 6x6 Pinzgauer GS platform has also been operationally trialed by UKSF. The fully independent suspension, high ground clearance, and five-cylinder turbocharged engine contribute to a vehicle that is ideally suited for the harsh terrain of Afghanistan. The SOV was first seen on the NZ SAS's 2005 tour, replacing a number of borrowed GMV-S used in earlier deployments.

This NZ SAS model features a 40mm Heckler & Koch GMG grenade launcher in the central mount and both forward- and rear-mounted FN MAG 58 GPMGs. Delta models currently mount the US Mk 47 Striker automatic grenade launcher (AGL) and Mk 48 GPMGs, whilst both also carry the M2 Browning. The vehicle illustrated features a pair of reloads for a Javelin ATGM launcher along with extensive fuel, water, and ammunition supplies for extended operations.

2: PERENTIE LONG RANGE PATROL VEHICLE (LRPV): 1 SQUADRON, SPECIAL AIR SERVICE REGIMENT (SASR), AFGHANISTAN, 2001

The venerable Australian Perentie is a unique design in the annals of Special Forces vehicles – a six-wheeler Land Rover custom-made for the Australian SASR. As implied by its name – after an Australian lizard – it was originally envisioned for long-range patrolling in Australia's arid outback, the Perentie has since been deployed as an offensive-action platform in Afghanistan and Iraq. Perhaps surprisingly, the LRPV was not deployed to East Timor as it was felt that the vehicle had become a signifier of the involvement of the SASR and betrayed the unit's otherwise low-profile presence.

Perenties are armed with a mixture of the M2 Browning and Mk 19 grenade launchers (being replaced by the H&K GMG system) and a forward-mounted FN MAG 58. They routinely mount a reconnaissance trail bike on the tailgate. Recent versions have been upgraded with an anti-mine protection kit after the tragic death of an SASR sergeant in Afghanistan in 2002.

1

2

Australian SASR patrol in Afghanistan riding Kawasaki trail bikes for route reconnaissance ahead of Perentie LRPVs. (Courtesy ADF SOCOMD)

introduced on the Polaris Sportsman MV (Military Version), which was adopted by USSOCOM. Some quads were even armed. The Czech Special Operations Group (SOG) that deployed in support of OEF mounted a Soviet-built AGS-17 AGL on the bed of at least one of its ATVs and photos exist of a US ODA Polaris mounting an unidentified recoilless rifle, although such a configuration was far more the exception than the rule.

In addition, the ODAs increasingly found motorcycles to be well suited to the often rough terrain of the region. ODAs, and their Coalition allies in UKSF and SASR, favor these for reconnaissance tasks or for getting into locations that a larger GMV or ATV simply could not negotiate. Bikes and ATVs also act as flank screens for SOF convoys, kicking up less dust and being able to extricate themselves more quickly from trouble than the larger patrol vehicles. Furthermore, the lightweight footprint of the motorcycles means that they are less likely to trigger Soviet-legacy mines. As with the ATVs, the bikes used by the SOF are modified for specialist use with mounting brackets for M4 carbines, enhanced suspensions, exhaust mufflers, and IR headlights.

Motorcycle models deployed by the ODAs are now almost exclusively made by Kawasaki, and include the KLR650 and the Army-issue M1030. The UK, Australia, and other Coalition SOF also use the modified Yamaha XT600 and various Honda 250 models. The Rangers also use the Kawasaki KLR250, modified to accept diesel, and the tiny Suzuki DS80 which is small enough to be strapped to the planks on the sides of an MH-6 Little Bird helicopter or stowed in the rear of a GMV or Ranger Special Operations Vehicle (RSOV – see below).

Pink Panthers, Bushmasters, and Perenties

UK Special Forces again deployed to Afghanistan with their old faithful, the DPV 110 Land Rover or Pink Panther/Pinkie, as it is still nicknamed. Continually refined in mobility training conducted in Africa and the Middle East, the DPVs were at both their zenith of operational capability and their expected service life, with a new vehicle intended as an eventual replacement waiting in the wings. Two squadrons of 22 SAS arrived in Afghanistan – A and G Squadrons – having recently conducted training exercises in Oman, in mid-October 2001.

After carrying out several largely uneventful SR operations, the squadrons returned to Hereford disappointed at the lack of missions allocated to them by the American command, before again deploying in December for Operation *Trent*, a mounted assault against a Taliban/al-Qaeda opium-processing plant. For this operation, the regiment deployed upwards of

40 vehicles, including DPVs armed with the M2 .50 HMGs, twin L7A2 GPMGs, Milan anti-tank guided missiles (ATGMs), and Mk 19 grenade launchers. The successful assault (detailed in Osprey Elite 163: *Special Operations Forces in Afghanistan*) was the only known mounted operation of its type conducted by 22 SAS in Afghanistan using the venerable Pink Panther. In 2002, the regiment was tasked with build-up training for the invasion of Iraq, which would be the vehicle's last operational deployment before being replaced by the Supacat HMT, which would become known by its code name, the "Menacity".

The SAS's sister unit, the SBS, initially deployed with civilian, unmarked Land Rover Defenders and Land Cruisers, as detailed earlier, although several SBS Land Rover 110s were eventually flown into Bagram for longer-range reconnaissance operations. The SBS also made extensive use of the Polaris ATV. The Australian Special Forces Task Group (SFTG) deployed its own version of the modified Land Rover in the form of the Jaguar-Rover produced Perentie LRPV and its 110-based wagons, known as Surveillance Reconnaissance Vehicles (SRVs), which shared many features with the UK SAS Pink Panther.

The LRPV, however, is a unique design built specifically for SASR use. Based on the six-wheel-drive Land Rover Perentie design (named after an Australian lizard), the LRPV was adopted in the late 1980s and features a turbocharged four-cylinder diesel engine. For route reconnaissance, it carries a 250cc motorcycle mounted on the rear tailgate. A central ring mount is equipped with either the .50 M2 or 40mm Mk 19 and a passenger-side weapon mount carries a Fabrique Nationale MAG 58 GPMG.

Both the LRPV and SRV performed admirably on a large number of extended patrols, although the Australians tragically suffered their first casualty in February 2002 when an LRPV struck a Soviet-legacy anti-tank mine, killing a SASR sergeant and disabling the vehicle. The mine incident led directly to the installation of an anti-mine armor system known as the Survival Enhancement Kit (SEK) for the LRPV. The SEK consisted of under-floor armor plates and shock-absorbent seating to reduce the potential severity of wounds caused by mine and IED strikes. Tenix Defence carried out an overhaul of all SASR LRPVs and Commando SRVs in 2005 to increase their service life until replacement platforms could be sourced.

As the Australian commitment increased, the Bushmaster 4x4 Protected Mobility Vehicle (PMV) was deployed with the Reconstruction Task Force (RTF) in 2005. The vehicle was soon co-opted by the 4th Battalion, Royal Australian Regiment (4 RAR, now 2 Commando) component of the re-titled Special Operations Task Group (SOTG), as it provides a greater level of safety against mines and IEDs due to its V-shaped hull. The Bushmaster mounts an MAG 58 GPMG on

A blurred but unique image of an Australian Bushmaster in service with UKSF in Iraq. The UKSF Bushmasters have been extensively modified for their role as armored transport for strike teams with an up-armor package, bull-bar, extensive ECM and anti-IED suites, and CROWS RWS mounting the M2 .50 machine-gun. The Bushmaster IMV was used in preference to the UKSF HMT 400 Menacity platforms, as the IMV provides better all-round protection in an urban environment. (Photographer unknown)

A blurry image of the UKSF Menacity HMT 400 produced by Supacat. These Menacity platforms are being employed by the SBS in Afghanistan. Note the lack of doors, unlike the sister vehicle the M-WMIK Jackal, and provision for two spare tires. A range of weapon options are visible, including twin L7A2 GPMGs and a mix of .50 M2s and H&K GMGs. (Photographer unknown)

its turret ring and features mounts for up to two F89 machine-guns (an Australian variant of the Minimi/SAW) next to the rear roof-mounted troop hatches. A Common Remotely Operated Weapon Station (CROWS) is currently being deployed to replace the GPMG.

The Bushmaster can also carry nine fully equipped soldiers (increased to ten in later versions) or several litters for casualty evacuation, allowing greater flexibility than the SRVs that 4 RAR were generally operating in. As the Commando element of the SOTG became more focused on DA raids, whilst the SASR returned to conducting mostly SR tasks, the vehicle also better matched operational requirements by being able to move Commandos quickly and relatively stealthily up to target locations, whilst offering a counter to any IEDs encountered en route. The Bushmaster PMV became one of the first of the so-called Mine Resistant Ambush Protected (MRAP) vehicles to be deployed to Afghanistan and to be employed by SOF. The Bushmaster is considered a Class 1 MRAP under the US designation system, based on vehicle weight, size, and envisioned role.

The Supacats

As mentioned, the UKSF Pink Panther DPV was nearing the end of its operational life when it deployed to Afghanistan. Two tenders dating back to the late 1990s had been opened by the UK Ministry of Defence for replacement vehicles for the UKSF fleet. These were known officially as the Surveillance and Reconnaissance Vehicle (SRV) and the Offensive Action Vehicle (OAV) programs. The tenders were eventually combined and the UK-based Supacat firm was announced as the winner with an initial order for 65 vehicles placed.

 D **SUPACAT MENACITY HMT 400 SRV/OAV: MOBILITY TROOP, B SQUADRON, 22 SPECIAL AIR SERVICE REGIMENT, AFGHANISTAN, 2009**

Codenamed the "Menacity," but officially known as the Surveillance and Reconnaissance Vehicle/Offensive Action Vehicle (SRV/OAV), this Supacat-produced design was first introduced into UKSF service in 2003–04. Versions of the platform were later purchased by the US Army's Delta, Danish Special Operations Forces (SOF), and the Australian Special Air Service Regiment (SASR), where it is known as the Nary. It was also later developed into the Mobility Weapon-Mounted Installation Kit (M-WMIK) Jackal and Jackal 2 for general service with the British Army.

The illustration shows an earlier version without the up-armoring now rumored to equip UKSF versions. The vehicle lacks the forward doors and appliqué armour package recognizable from the Jackal version and features a triple smoke discharger mount on either side of the crew cabin rather than the four mount on the Jackal. It also features two spare tires versus the single generally carried on non-SF versions. It is armed with a Browning M2 .50 in the turret mount, fitted with an EOTech Holographic Weapons Sight, and a forward-mounted L7A2 GPMG at the passenger position.

The vehicle illustrated is heavily loaded for extended operations both in terms of supplies and extra weapons and ammunition. Note the fuel carried in the rear bustle racks and the Javelin ATGM strapped to the top hamper.

A detailed frontal view of a UK M-WMIK Jackal based on the UKSF Menacity Supacat HMT. It has many of the same features as the SF version, such as the mounted H&K GMG and forward L7A2 GPMG. Of particular interest is the tow rope, fitted for immediate use, and the bolt-on up-armor package not seen on the original SF variants. (Courtesy Pete Gill)

The winning design, codenamed the Menacity, was the Supacat HMT 400, a 4x4 with improved payload and cross-country capabilities compared to the DPV and which was fully transportable within a CH-47 Chinook. The SAS and SBS began receiving their first SRV/OAV vehicles in 2003. UKSF Supacat SRV/OAVs offer an adjustable ride height through a central tire inflation system, allowing the vehicle to negotiate difficult terrain; this system has already proven itself in Afghanistan. It also features a payload capacity of up to 1½ tons and a top road speed of more than 120km/h (75mph), being powered by a six-cylinder turbocharged diesel engine. UKSF versions feature run-flat tires, IR headlights, and a range of weapon options on the central ring mount, including the M2 .50, twin L7A2 GPMGs, and the Heckler & Koch Grenade Machine-Gun (GMG) along with a forward passenger mounted L7A2 GPMG.

Following the operational success of the UKSF version, the regular British Army has itself also adopted the HMT 400 platform as the Mobility Weapon-Mounted Installation Kit (M-WMIK) or Jackal light patrol vehicle to replace the Land Rover-based Wolf WMIKs. An upgraded version, known as Jackal 2, is currently being procured with an improved armor protection suite and reinforced chassis. It is unknown at the time of writing if UKSF vehicles will receive similar modifications.

A promotional image of an NZ SAS patrol in Afghanistan, 2005, utilizing the Pinzgauer 6x6 SOV with .50 M2 mounting an EOTech sight. Of interest is the AT-4 (M136) rocket behind the turret gunner, the empty rear weapons mount (normally carrying an FN MAG 58), and the multiple smoke dischargers mounted at each corner of the vehicle. (Courtesy New Zealand Defence Force)

The British Army wasn't the only organization watching the UKSF purchase of the HMT 400 with interest. The US JSOC, through its parent organization, USSOCOM, ordered 47 of the HMT 400 SRV/OAVs based on the successful UKSF design. These vehicles were destined for Delta to supplement its Pinzgauer 6x6 Special Operations Vehicles, NSTVs, GMVs, and 6x6 Pandur armored vehicles. Denmark also purchased 15 of the HMT 4x4E Extenda version for its SOF – the Extenda can reasonably quickly add a third axle, thus becoming a 6x6 platform with greater payload capacity.

The Australian LRPV, like its British counterpart, was beginning to show its age and a replacement was sought by the Australian Army's Special Operations Command (SOCOMD). In 2006, an order was placed with Supacat for 31 of the HMT 400 vehicles based on the UKSF SRV/OAV version but with some slight variations, such as in the arrangement of the smoke-grenade launchers (Australian HMTs feature six launchers versus the eight on UKSF versions, for unknown reasons) and a squared top hamper surrounding the weapon ring mount (shared with the Danish version).

The Australian version was christened the Nary Special Operations Vehicle (SOV), in memory of an Australian SASR warrant officer killed in pre-Iraq SOTG build-up training. Although ordered in 2006, the Narys are only set to debut operationally to Uruzgan Province, southern Afghanistan, in late 2011. Initial feedback on the performance of the platform by SASR operators has focused on the lack of mine/IED protection, leading to speculation that the vehicles may receive an armor upgrade in a similar fashion to the Jackal 2 recently adopted by the British Army.

The 6x6 version of the HMT, now being purchased by the British as the Coyote, has also been purchased by the Australian SASR, although it is currently unknown if this is the Supacat 4x4 Extenda version, which can be converted to a 6x6 configuration, or the dedicated HMT 600 Coyote.

Dune Buggies, IFAVs, RSOVs, and Strykers

Along with their inherited HMMWVs, the SEALs deployed a number of their M1040 and M1041 DPV dune buggies, which were used during several sensitive site exploitation operations, often inserted via sling load under a Chinook. The DPV, produced by racing firm Chenowth, is powered by a Porsche Racing four-cylinder engine and can reach speeds of up to 130km/h (81mph) on paved roads. It also carries an impressive weapons load, with either a 40mm Mk 19 or .50 M2 on a mount at the top of the frame, a passenger mount for an M60E3 or M240B, and a rear-facing mount, again for an M60E3 or M240B. Additionally, there are mounting brackets provided for AT-4 anti-tank rockets to give the SEALs a limited anti-armor punch.

The DPVs' performance in Afghanistan was by all accounts rather mixed, with the vehicle often encountering issues with the terrain (according to SEAL participants, its rear-wheel drive was useless in soft sand) and its limited fuel capacity and inability to use diesel were further problems. The DPV was, however, famously deployed on the covert operation to transfer captured HVT and 9/11 planner Khalid Sheikh Mohammed from Pakistan across the border into southern Afghanistan. Rangers and elements of the 504th Parachute Infantry parachuted in to secure a dry riverbed in Jawsani so as to enable an MC-130 transport plane to land. SEALs from the Tier One Naval Special Warfare Development Group (DEVGRU) appeared from across the border in a three-seat DPV with the HVT strapped into the rear seat. The DPV drove up the rear ramp of the MC-130 and the Hercules taxied and took off, transporting the HVT into CIA custody.

The Marines of Force Recon, now largely subsumed into the recently formed Special Operations Battalions of Marine Special Operations Command (MARSOC), arrived in Afghanistan in late 2001 with their Interim Fast Attack Vehicle (IFAV), based on the Mercedes G-Wagen 290 GDT 4x4. The IFAV is crewed by three Marines and is armed with a Mk 19 or an M2 on a pedestal mount and a forward passenger mount M249 or M240. Although the vehicle was initially deployed as a soft-skin, it was quickly up-armored with a light armor kit in-theater. With the increasing IED threat, movement of Marines has been largely taken up by a number of MRAP platforms, with the IFAVs relegated to limited mission-specific tasks.

The US Army Rangers deployed early to Afghanistan and have maintained a presence there for most of the conflict, often acting as the DA support element for whichever Special Mission Unit (SMU) is currently rotated in as the lead unit in the HVT hunt. In the 2001–02 timeframe, the Rangers used the early GMV and their specialist Land Rover design, the Ranger Special Operations Vehicle (RSOV).

The RSOV was developed by the Rangers as a direct replacement for their aging M151 gun trucks. A principal reason for the adoption of the RSOV was that the it can be driven into MH-47 Chinook or MH-53 Pave Low

E **M1040 CHENOWTH DESERT PATROL VEHICLE: SEAL TEAM FOUR, AFGHANISTAN, 2002**

The M1040 Desert Patrol Vehicle (DPV) is the famous armed dune buggy of the Navy SEALs. Although a similar vehicle was trialed and dismissed by UKSF in Operation *Desert Storm*, the Chenowth DPV found some favor with the SEALs, although they acknowledge the many limits of the dune buggy. This example illustrates a vehicle deployed during a sensitive site exploitation operation at Tarnak Farms Two, a former al-Qaeda training facility in Afghanistan, in 2002.

The three-seat DPV mounts a 40mm Mk19 automatic grenade launcher and forward- and rear-mounted 7.62x51mm Mk 43 Mod 0 machine-guns (the updated version of the M60E3). Also carried are two M136 (AT-4) rockets. As the vehicle cannot carry heavy weights in sandy environments without a greater risk of bogging, this DPV is mainly devoid of stowage apart from the patrol day sacks of the crew strapped to the frame.

An *aide-memoire* for the "nine-liner" – the format used to call in medical evacuation for wounded service members – taped against the communications stand for instant use inside an Army GMV-S. (Courtesy Rob Skipper)

An exceptionally rare image of an NZ SAS patrol mounted in a Pinzgauer 6x6 SOV on long-range patrol operations in Afghanistan, along with a passing camel! The SOV mounts a .50 M2 and forward and rear FN MAG 58 GPMGs. Also just visible is a Kawasaki dirt bike carried on the vehicle for route reconnaissance. The SOV is also utilized by Delta and was amongst some of the first vehicles to be air-dropped into Afghanistan in October 2001 and to cross the border in the 2003 invasion of Iraq. (Author's photo)

helicopters, which cannot be done with the majority of HMMWV variants, due to their dimensions. The RSOV is based on the turbocharged, four-cylinder, diesel-powered 110 Land Rover Defender, and is deployed in several variants including: the standard RSOV (which mounts an M240B on a passenger weapons mount and has a rear turret ring mounting either the Mk 19 or M2); the MEDSOV medical version, which can carry up to six casualties on litters; a command-and-control variant known as the C2SOV, and the mortar carrier MORTSOV, to support the Rangers' integral 120mm mortar capability.

One company of each Ranger battalion is equipped with the RSOV, with the vehicle being deployed on the basis of four vehicles per platoon, split into a pair of two vehicle squads with one vehicle mounting the M2 and the other the Mk 19. The RSOV also carries AT-4 light anti-tank rockets, Javelin ATGM, and the Ranger-specific Carl Gustav M3 84mm recoilless rifle, giving the mounted Rangers an anti-armor capability.

The RSOV admirably fulfilled the regiment's need for an armed tactical transport platform to support its traditional site seizure and exploitation missions with heavy weapon platforms. Yet the vehicle lacked the capability for long-range desert operations as performed by Delta and 22 SAS in Iraq's western desert during both *Desert Storm* and *Iraqi Freedom*. For these, the Rangers selected the GMV in the form of a variant known as the GMV-R (R for Ranger), which was also specifically developed for the Ranger Regiment but physically appears similar to the GMV-S Special Forces version.

In their 2005 deployment to Afghanistan in support of the Joint Special Operations Task Force

(JSOTF), the 75th Rangers made a request for the loan of some 14 M1126 Stryker Infantry Carrier Vehicles (ICVs), an M1133 Medical Evacuation Vehicle, and an M1130 Command Vehicle. Combined with the Rangers' use of Delta's Pandur Armored Ground Mobility System (AGMS) and joint operations in Iraq with the Stryker Brigade Combat Teams (BCTs), the "temporary" loan (there is currently no fixed date for return of the vehicles) gives the Rangers a protected transportation capability for road movement or indeed direct-action operations against Taliban compounds. It is understood that the Rangers have extensively modified the vehicles to suit their unique mission requirements (almost certainly including the latest generation of anti-IED electronic countermeasures suites), but exact details of such modifications are rightly classified.

Other Coalition SOF in Afghanistan

A large number of other NATO and non-NATO member states have contributed troops to either the American OEF or NATO ISAF mission in Afghanistan. Many of these contributions have included SOF. Coverage of every vehicle used by contributing nations' SOF is impossible given the large number, but several of the more interesting and unusual vehicles deserve mention.

The NZ SAS initially deployed in borrowed HMMWVs, but in its 2005 deployment brought with it a number of Pinzgauer 6x6 Special Operations Vehicles (SOVs) from a purchase of 13 vehicles. These SOVs, also used by Delta and in limited numbers by 22 SAS, are based on the Model 712 and are capable of carrying an off-road payload of nearly 1,500kg (3,300lb), have a range of some 700km (435 miles), and feature a center-mount weapons station and both forward and rear machine-gun mounts.

Norway deployed its Jegerkommando and Marine-Jegerkommando in early 2002, known collectively as Norwegian Special Operations Forces (NORSOF). For the Afghan mission under Task Force K-Bar, NORSOF used 4x4 Mercedes 290 G-Wagens with extensive modifications and mounting an M2 .50 HMG. In fact, the Mercedes G-Wagen platform was one of the most common platforms for European Coalition SOF – the German Kommando-Spezialkräfte (KSK), the Dutch Korps Commandotroepen (KCT, also known as Viper, working alongside SASR), and the Danish Jægerkorps all utilized versions of the vehicle before later deploying GMV-style HMMWVs.

The KSK, and Canada's JTF-2, were forced to use loaned US HMMWVs before their own vehicles arrived. The KSK operators quickly went to work on their borrowed vehicles, taking off the doors and windscreens of the M1038 Cargo HMMWVs to allow the operators to fire outward if caught in an ambush (the KSK also

A Czech SOG Toyota Hilux in Afghanistan with up-armor kit from the Czech company SVOS. Note the bustle-rack equipped turret with twin weapon systems – an AGS-17 30mm AGL and a co-located 7.62x54mm PKM, which appears to have been fitted with an EOTech-style Holographic Weapons Sight. (Courtesy SOG)

Polish GROM operating in Afghanistan in borrowed GMVs from the 2nd Battalion, 3rd Special Forces Group. Note the unusually mounted spare wheel adorned with animal skull and the M136 (AT-4) anti-tank rocket strapped next to the .50 gunner. GROM also utilizes custom Hilux and Land Rover Defenders. (Courtesy GROM)

stirred some minor controversy by allegedly using stenciled Afrika Korps symbols on these vehicles).

The KSK has since adopted the G-Wagen-based Rheinmetall AGF Serval Special Operations Vehicle, which incorporates many GMV-style innovations, including a swing-arm mounted MG3 machine-gun, smoke dischargers, and permanent satellite communications antennae. The vehicle also features a center-mount weapons ring for a .50 HMG or Heckler & Koch 40mm GMG grenade launcher. The Serval can be transported by German CH-53 helicopters and thus also US MH-53s by lowering the hinged weapons ring in much the same way as with the ECV GMV.

The Polish Grupa Reagowania Operacyjno Manewrowego (Operational Mobile Reaction Group or GROM) also deployed with GMV-style HMMWVs, whilst the Italian Col Moschin SF use WMIK-style Land Rover 90 Defenders with ring-mounted M2 or Mk 19 weapons. The French Commandement des Opérations Spéciales (Special Operations Command or COS) deployed a limited number of the 4x4 Panhard Véhicule Patrouille Spéciale (VPS), based on the G-Wagen.

OPERATION *IRAQI FREEDOM*

An Overview

The invasion of Iraq in March 2003 presented Coalition SOF with a differing set of challenges from those experienced during OEF in Afghanistan. In support of conventional forces, SOF would again act as the spearhead, carrying out a range of operations across the country. To the north, Combined Joint Special Operations Task Force – North (CJSOTF-N), otherwise known as Task Force Viking, was formed around the 10th Special Forces Group and 3/3rd Special Forces Group supported by the 173rd Airborne and elements of the 10th Mountain Division. Their role was originally to support the 4th Infantry Division's attack south from Turkey. When Turkey denied basing rights to Coalition forces, the soldiers of Task Force Viking went from being a supporting command to being a supported command and leading the invasion from the north.

The 10th Special Forces Group was not one of the traditional "mobility"-based SF Groups (5th and 3rd are routinely equipped with GMVs as part of their table of organization and equipment) and thus were forced to improvise by purchasing some 236 NSTVs made up of 206 Land Rover Defenders with modifications (in a mix of civilian colors, but many painted white) in a job lot direct from Land Rover Solihull, England, and 30 Toyota Tacomas from dealerships in Germany. These Defenders and Tacomas were fitted with rollbars and weapons mounts that allowed M240s and Mk 19s to be deployed. The 3rd luckily brought its GMVs and "War Pigs" (essentially armed resupply trucks – see below pages 36–37) with it; these vehicles were soon put to good use at the battle of the Debecka Pass.

This operation, known as *Northern Safari*, saw several ODAs and a small number of Kurdish Peshmerga allies attempting to hold a strategic pass overlooking a central crossroad leading to Mosul and Kirkuk. Attacked by Iraqi Army MTLB armored personnel carriers (APCs) and later T-55 main battle tanks (MBTs), the Special Forces engaged with their GMV-mounted

Mk 19s and M2s to buy time to deploy their Javelin anti-tank missiles. The Javelin proved supremely effective and stalled the armored attack until US Navy fast air support could be summoned to destroy the Iraqi T-55s, which had managed to hide behind a sand

A 5th Special Forces Group early-model GMV-S in March 2003 in Iraq's western deserts. It carries both the M2 .50 and swing-arm M240B 7.62x51mm and has been finished in a hand-painted camouflage pattern. An orange aerial VS-17 Identification Friend or Foe (IFF) indicator has been affixed to the rear – a necessary safety device when operating far forward of friendly troops. (Courtesy Rob C)

berm and thus beyond targeting by the line-of-sight Javelin.

To the northwest of Task Force Viking operated two UKSF task forces known collectively as Task Force 7 – one half formed from B and D Squadrons, 22 SAS, and the other from C Squadron of the SBS. Mounted in their faithful Pinkie DPVs, the UKSF elements conducted a "Scud hunt" for Saddam's Scud B missile launchers and conducted raids and interdiction operations against Iraqi units. These would be amongst the last major operations for the DPVs as they were in the process, noted earlier, of being retired and replaced by the new Supacat design.

Whilst 22 SAS helped seize a strategic airfield known as H-2, the SBS element ran into trouble. On March 24, an SBS mobility patrol, deployed near Mosul, was ambushed by what has been variously reported as a large force of Bedouin or an Iraqi anti-SOF patrol, causing a frantic effort to break contact. RAF Special Forces Flight Chinooks flew in from Jordan to exfiltrate the patrol but not before a Pinkie, an ATV, and a motorcycle were abandoned by the retreating SBS – the vehicles were soon filmed and the images broadcast on al-Jazeera. Also left behind in the confusion were two SBS operators, who were forced to conduct a terrifying 160km (100-mile) escape and evasion on a Polaris ATV with AC-130 gunships, Navy fast air, and Predator unmanned aerial vehicles (UAVs) flying top cover for the pair all the way to the Syrian border.

Another view of a 5th Special Forces "War Pig," again illustrating just how much these unique vehicles can carry. Visible behind the crew are numerous antennae for different communications sets, including the Single-Channel Ground–Air Radio System (SINGARS). Also visible is the forward-mounted M240B and the centrally mounted 40mm Mk 19 with thermal sight. (Courtesy Rob C)

In the south, SEALs and Polish GROM from the Naval Special Operations Task Group conducted seizure operations against the Iraqi port of Umm Qasr, two off-shore platforms, and the al-Faw Manifold, where the SEALs deployed their dune buggy DPVs. Also to the south, ODAs mounted in GMVs and attached SAS patrols in DPVs assisted the advance of the British 1st Armoured Division into Basra in the south, conducting recce, screening, and raiding missions.

An Iraqi SF HMMWV complete with ASK turret and 7.62x54mm PKM GPMG. The camouflage net, possibly IR-treated, is applied to conceal the silhouette of the turret gunner as an anti-sniper measure. Note also the flashing police light mounted upon the CREW IED jammer and the additional directional spotlight. (Courtesy Rob Skipper)

To the west, Task Force 20, known as the Wolverines and comprising a Delta squadron supported by members of 3/75th Ranger Battalion, became the first US SOF to cross the border, in the pre-dawn darkness on March 19, 2003. Task Force 20's key missions included seizing high-value sites such as H-1 and H-3 airfields and the Haditha Dam complex, along with cutting Highway 1 and conducting deception operations and raids to confuse Iraqi understanding of the Coalition's strategic intentions. The deception missions led to the deploymnt of one of the most unusual vehicles to feature in any SOF task force – the M1A1 Abrams MBT.

Also operating in the west of Iraq was the 5th Special Forces Group-based Combined Joint Special Operations Task Force – West (CJSOTF-W) – better known as Task Force Dagger, a codename from the opening days of the Afghan campaign. Dagger, operating in GMVs, War Pigs, and NSTVs, was tasked to conduct the hunt for Scuds in a similar fashion to the missions conducted by them a decade earlier in the 1991 Gulf War. In addition, they carried out long-range vehicle- and helicopter-insertion SR missions, site seizures, and screening operations to ascertain Iraqi forces' strength and dispositions. Alongside the Green Berets operated the largest Allied SOF component under Dagger command – the UKSF of Task Force 7 and the Australians of Task Force 64.

Despite the massive and lengthy preparations for the invasion of Iraq, some units still hadn't had suitable vehicles supplied when they crossed the border. The Recon Marines of 1st Reconnaissance Battalion, for instance, now immortalized in the book and television series *Generation Kill*, were forced to rely upon standard M998 and M1025 HMMWVs, which they customized themselves in-theater. A bare handful of early up-armored kits were made available, as were a limited pool of M1114s. The SEALs too, as described earlier, had to make do with less-than-optimal vehicles when they deployed to Baghdad following the seizure of the al-Faw pipeline. For others, perhaps those with more experience in mobility operations, the right equipment was largely in place.

After the invasion, the requirements for SOF vehicles in-theater gradually changed with the advent of the largely urban insurgency in Iraq. The IED- and RPG-initiated ambush became the key tactic of the insurgents, with the IEDs growing in size and sophistication as the Coalition responded with both tactical and technological innovations to combat them, spearheaded by the Joint IED Defeat Organization (JIEDDO). With a lack of up-armored patrol vehicles in 2003 and 2004, SOF units were forced to improvise by scavenging metal plate to be fashioned by unit mechanics into makeshift armor for their GMVs until up-armoring kits and larger numbers of M1114s became available.

Technology was quickly brought into play in the battle against the bombers. Many of the anti-IED systems remain classified, but some of the older systems deployed on Coalition SOF vehicles can be described in very general terms. The CREW and SYMPHONY IED jammers have been widely used to prevent the initiation of radio-controlled IEDs. They

A US Army SF ECV GMV-S on operations in Iraq. This example, and its partner in the background, features a bull-bar complete with additional light mounts and a spotlight slaved to the .50 M2, along with additional ammunition bins mounted externally on the turret for instant access. An M4 carbine is often clip-mounted inside the turret in case of a main weapon stoppage or to engage close-in targets below the elevation arc of the .50 machine-gun. (Courtesy Rob Skipper)

work by disrupting the frequencies used by common IED initiators such as car alarms and mobile phones. The CREW, for instance, has been seen both on MRAPs and GMVs and appears as a pole-mounted mushroom-style device. The drawback of the technological systems for jamming IED frequencies is that they are largely non-selective, meaning that the interference will affect Coalition communications and IEDs alike.

Along with jamming systems, other innovations such as the Vehicle Optics Sensor System (VOSS) have been fitted to USSOCOM RG-31 MRAPs. The VOSS is a pole-mounted camera that offers magnified daytime, IR, and thermal modes to allow the crew to scan for IEDs in any environment from a safe stand-off distance. Other passive anti-IED technologies include the HUSKY Mounted Detection System, designed to counter pressure-plate initiated IEDs by providing a ground-penetrating radar capability to locate buried devices, and the hugely successful RHINO II and III, which use a boom-mounted heat source to disrupt the IR beams used to trigger the deadly EFP IEDs and detonate them prematurely.

The insurgents have responded to these innovations by revising both their tactics and the types of IEDs they are building. EFPs, for example, are now offset to allow for RHINO booms, but the Coalition has responded with variable boom lengths. The success of jamming devices has led to a return to rudimentary pressure-plate or command-wire initiated devices in some areas, both techniques that expose the IED and its planters to a greater risk of discovery as they emplace or attempt to detonate the device. The jihadists of al-Qaeda have increasingly been forced to rely on vehicle-borne IEDs (VBIEDs) or suicide bombers to deliver their devices as the anti-IED countermeasures have made traditional devices much more difficult to employ.

The Pandurs, Team Tank, and the War Pigs

Delta, perhaps incorporating lessons learnt in the 1993 battle of the Black Sea in Mogadishu, Somalia, ordered the AGMS through USSOCOM in 2000. Although the contract with General Dynamics Land Systems was for up to 50 AGMS vehicles, it is understood that only 12 were actually purchased. The vehicle is a custom-built variant of the General Dynamics/Steyr Pandur 6x6 platform and can carry up to seven soldiers along with a crew consisting of driver and commander. The Delta version features a six-cylinder, 6.6-liter engine, a roof weapons mount for a .50 machine-gun or 40mm AGL, including an ASK-type gun shield, and has been modified with the addition

A patrol of USSOCOM RG-33 series 4x4 Mine Protected Vehicles (MPVs) in Iraq manned by members of the CJSOTF-AP and equipped with CROWS II RWSs mounting M2 .50 machine-guns. (Courtesy US Navy; photo by Petty Officer 1st Class Joseph W. Pfaff)

of custom up-armoring, firing ports, and a MOWAG Piranha-style driver's compartment with ballistic glass.

Delta deployed these vehicles both in the initial ground invasion of Iraq and later in the counterinsurgency campaign during the hunt for HVTs and insurgent bombmakers and logisticians. AGMSs were also seen at the rescue of Private Jessica Lynch, along with several GMV-Ss, used by the ground insertion force. The Pandur AGMS provided a similar capability to that of the Strykers officially loaned to the 75th Ranger Regiment in 2005 for its Afghan deployment – it is a relatively quiet, fast, and armored transport vehicle that could withstand, or at least reduce, the blast effects from IEDs. The vehicle also provides the off-road versatility of a 6x6 platform and an impressive range of some 650km (404 miles). USSOCOM is apparently happy with the Pandur, as it purchased a further 11 units in 2006, again destined for the Special Mission Units (SMUs) of JSOC.

At the time of the purchase, USSOCOM explained: "Special operations forces operate in small teams. And recent experiences in crisis locations around the world have shown that special operations forces need this kind of a vehicle – for its mobility and its protection. This type of vehicle will give the special operations force units the capability to escort humanitarian relief convoys, to help patrol outlying areas, and otherwise operate in high threat environments." Whilst one may wonder how many humanitarian relief convoys Delta will be escorting, the point is well made that the Pandur provides a protected movement capability for the SMUs.

Delta's Task Force Wolverine entered Iraq in a mix of Pandurs, 6x6 Pinzgauer SOVs, GMV-S HMMWVs, and NSTVs, along with a range of quad Polaris ATVs and motorbikes. As an example of the vehicle-mounted operations conducted by the Wolverines, Delta's C Squadron in Pinzgauers and three platoons of Rangers in 14 GMV-Rs and four M998 Cargo HMMWVs assaulted and captured the Haditha Dam complex on April 1, 2003. Delta moved on toward Tikrit and engaged in a running gun battle with a large force of Iraqi fedayeen irregulars in technicals that had been shadowing them (and which Delta engaged with Javelin ATGMs carried on its Pinzgauers). Meanwhile, the Rangers held the dam for five days against numerous enemy counterattacks. The Pinzgauer SOV proved popular with Delta and the Rangers, resulting in a further purchase of an unspecified number of vehicles by JSOC in April 2007.

The Wolverines also called on the services of a truck-mounted High-Mobility Artillery Rocket System (HIMARS), which delivered both direct and indirect fire-support by launching either volleys of six unguided rockets or one larger guided missile loaded with bomblets; the HIMARS fired in support of the Task Force 20 seizure of Haditha Dam. Furthermore, C Company, 2/70th Armor, was tasked on April 2 to link up with the SOF task force at H-1 airfield before forward-deploying to a desert airstrip known as Mission Support Site Grizzly. The armor then conducted operations under the command of the Delta squadron commander. Ten M1A1 Abrams MBTs, an M981 FIST-V fire-support vehicle, three M113 APCs, and several fuel and cargo trucks were flown forward by C-17 Globemaster cargo aircraft.

"Team Tank," as the armored force was soon christened, was involved in numerous raiding, deception, and interdiction missions with Delta and the Rangers. The use of attached heavy armor by an SOF unit deep behind enemy lines (Delta had also accomplished one of the longest infiltrations into enemy territory in history) was a first and the mission succeeded admirably. Fearing they faced an armored division, the Iraqi leadership came to believe that the Coalition's main attack would occur from the west rather than the south.

In one memorable operation, Delta and Team Tank carried out a night-time deception raid on the outskirts of Saddam Hussein's home town of

The only known publicly released image of the elusive Pandur AGMS 6x6 deployed by Delta in Iraq. First introduced in March 2000, the vehicles all feature the unique ballistic glass protected driver's shield and ASK-style Mk 64 gun turrets. Note also the evidence for the custom passive appliqué up-armor kit bolted to the chassis and the multitude of antennae for differing radios and several mounted ECM and anti-IED devices. (Courtesy of US Department of Defense)

A clear close-up view of an Army SF GMV-S mounting the distinctive rear tray up-armor kit. Note the anti-IED jammer and running boards, the latter often used for mounted approaches to target locations. (Courtesy Rob Skipper)

The rocket rack of a HIMARS mounted on an FMTV truck as deployed by Task Force 20 in the western Iraqi desert in 2003 and later in Afghanistan with Task Force 373. Fully air transportable by C-130, the HIMARS provided the SF operators with indirect artillery fire support far outside the artillery envelope of advancing Coalition forces. (Courtesy Rob Skipper)

Tikrit, engaging *fedayeen* irregulars in technicals with the Abrams' 120mm main guns before withdrawing under the covering fire from MH-60 Direct Action Penetrator (DAP) helicopter gunships of the 1/160th Special Operations Aviation Regiment (SOAR). The deployment of Team Tank was not, however, without its problems. A Ranger GMV was accidentally engaged by one of the tanks during a contact with Iraqi forces, tragically killing an attached 24th Special Tactics Squadron (STS) combat controller. A Team Tank M1A1 also drove into a hole during a night operation, injuring a member of the crew and resulting in the vehicle having to be destroyed later by two main gun rounds from a sister tank.

In the immediate build-up to the invasion, the 5th and 3rd Special Forces Groups were busy updating an old concept for the 21st century. The mobility specialists secured a number of 2½-ton M1078 Light Medium Tactical Vehicles (LMTVs), license-built versions of the Austrian Steyr 12M18 produced by the US firm of Stewart & Stevenson Tactical Vehicles Systems for a new role.

Based on the "mother-ship" idea of mobile resupply pioneered by both the SAS and LRDG in World War II, and later by 22 SAS in the 1991 Gulf War, the LMTVs were stripped down and rebuilt from the ground up. The suspension springs were replaced; the cab was cut off creating a completely open-top vehicle; a centerline heavy weapons mount was bolted to the floor to accommodate an M2 or Mk 19; swing-arm mounts were added on the passenger side and rear to carry M240s; radio mounts were added for satellite radios, which could be left permanently deployed for instant use; and bustle racks for jerry cans, ammunition, and other supplies were added.

The "War Pigs" (named evidently in honor of the Black Sabbath song of the same name) were operated by Operational Detachment Bravos (ODBs), which provide command-and-control and facilitate resupply for the ODAs operating in their GMVs and NSTVs. In practice, the War Pigs allowed SF teams to operate for far longer in the field by rendezvousing with the vehicles for replenishment without recourse to potentially risky helicopter resupply.

Another variant of the War Pig concept was developed later by ODAs operating south of Baghdad during the insurgency – an M1083 5-ton cargo truck with armor plating (so-called "hillbilly armor"), a forward ring-mounted M240 and a pair of forward- and rear-mounted swing-arm M240s. The 5-ton War Pig was used as a field expedient transport for mixed ODA and Iraqi SOF raiding teams and as a gun truck to provide massive amounts of suppressive fire. It also carried Javelin launchers and the Carl Gustav M3 84mm for engaging enemy strongpoints in buildings.

The Evolution of the GMV

Drawing from the recent lessons from Afghanistan, the 5th Special Forces Group continued to refine the GMV concept and deployed large numbers of GMVs in the western deserts of Iraq during the invasion. Ironically, the majority of 5th Group's GMVs were still deployed in Afghanistan with the 3rd SF Group, and the 5th was forced to refit standard HMMWVs to GMV configuration before its Iraq deployment.

Since the start of the Iraq War, the GMV has been refined into a complete family of custom SOF-specific HMMWVs – the GMV-S for the Special Forces, the GMV-R for the Rangers, the GMV-N for the SEALs and the GMV-M for MARSOC. It is understood that USAF Special Operations Command have also purchased a number of GMV variants for its Special Tactics (ST) operators – the GMV-T Mobility Training Vehicle; the GMV-SD for the "black" (i.e. covert) JSOC-tasked 24th STS; and the GMV-ST for the "white" (i.e. non-covert) STS.

Many of the later production GMVs were based on the M1113 Enhanced Capacity Vehicle (ECV) variant, which offers: a heavier chassis and increased payload; a new turbocharged, eight-cylinder 6.5-liter engine; and perhaps most crucially, a Military Systems Group (MSG) manufactured Low-Profile A-Frame weapons mount, which allows the vehicle to be transported inside the CH/MH-47 Chinook (although it is still a tight fit!) by lowering the overall height by 76mm (3in). As noted earlier, prior to development of the M1113 GMV, the vehicles had to be carried in a sling load under the helicopter.

The M1113 GMV version also adds a three-bay ammunition holder next to the main weapon and the option of a secondary weapons mount for an M240 or M249 along with smoke-grenade dischargers. Modular armor kits are now provided with the GMV to allow operators to assess the threat level for a specific operation and adjust the GMV's armor to match, including up-armored doors and half-doors and improved ballistic glass. The

A rare close-up of an M134 7.62x51mm minigun in Iraq, dating from 2003. The weapon is mounted in an early ASK turret on an US Army Special Forces up-armored HMMWV. The minigun-equipped HMMWVs were often used as a lead "gun truck" in a patrol convoy to suppress any ambushes immediately. (Courtesy Deuterium)

A 5th Special Forces Group War Pig, based on the 2½-ton M1078 LMTV, caught in a sandstorm in Iraq, March 2003. Of particular interest is the Mk 19 AGL mounting a thermal weapons sight and forward-mounted SATCOM array. Note also the Polaris MV700 ATV parked in front of the War Pig. (Courtesy Rob C)

vehicles have also been internally reinforced and blast-proofing added as an anti-mine/IED measure.

For the battle in Iraqi cities, SOF began not only to up-armor their vehicles, but also up-gun them to assist in suppressing the large mobs of insurgents they were increasingly encountering. GMVs appeared mounting M134 miniguns (generally only on the lead vehicle of a patrol) and twin M240 or Mk48 GPMGs. To assist with one of their primary missions, that of raiding, GMVs were further modified with winches and rams for forcing the gates or reinforced doors of target compounds.

An excellent side profile of a 5th Special Forces Group War Pig mounting an M2 .50 machine-gun. The vehicle's role as a mobile resupply point is well illustrated by the number of fuel cans in the rear bed; note also the collapsed casualty litter visible above the rear-mounted spare tires. (Courtesy Rob C)

As the post-invasion security situation deteriorated and insurgent use of IEDs increased, SOF augmented their GMVs with up-armored M1114 and M1152 HMMWVs, forsaking their custom vehicles for increased protection against roadside bombs and adding the aftermarket HMMWV Armored Demountable Kit (HArD) up-armoring kit and ASK gun shields and later the FRAG 6 kit incorporating the Objective Gunner Protection Kit (OGPK) with full 360-degree protection and ballistic glass equipped vision ports. Additionally, SOF began to replace their HMMWVs in many cases with the first of the MRAP platforms ordered by USSOCOM.

Covert Operations

Delta and 22 SAS were deployed later in the Iraqi counterinsurgency campaign as a key component of the JSOTF operating under various codenames such as Task Force 21 or 141 along with the SBS, Special Forces Support Group, the Special Reconnaissance Regiment, the Naval Special Warfare Development

  GROUND MOBILITY VEHICLE – SPECIAL FORCES (GMV-S) EARLY VERSION: OPERATIONAL DETACHMENT ALPHA, 5TH SPECIAL FORCES GROUP, IRAQ, 2003

Before the current Enhanced Capability Vehicle (ECV) versions of the GMV-S, based on the M1113 platform, GMVs were developed from standard but extensively modified M1025 models. This GMV is typical of the vehicles deployed during the initial years of Operation *Enduring Freedom* and the invasion of Iraq. As the threat of IEDs had yet to fully develop, speed and maneuverability were favored over armored protection. The forward doors on this GMV have been removed to allow easy egress and for the crew to fire their personal weapons from the interior (during the invasion phase of Operation *Iraqi Freedom*, ODA units commonly jury-rigged an M4, shotgun, or even captured submachine-guns like the Sterling or MP5 with bungee cord to the inner frame as a "car gun" for the driver). The massive amount of stowage indicates this vehicle is tasked with long-range patrols and SR missions in the western deserts as part of the Combined Joint Special Operations Task Force – Arabian Peninsula (formerly Task Force Dagger – Combined Joint Special Operations Task Force – West), spearheaded by the 5th Special Forces Group, and would have been principally resupplied by the War Pig LMTVs of the Operational Detachment Bravo (ODB) units.

This GMV mounts the venerable .50 M2 Browning heavy machine-gun with quick-change barrel in the turret position and an M240B 7.62x51mm machine-gun on the swing-arm mount at the passenger position. Note also the permanently mounted SATCOM radio antennae in the rear bed, partly hidden amongst the stowage.

One of the only known images of an Air Force Special Tactics GMV-ST. The GMV-ST appears even more stripped down than the SF version – this example lacks any doors or armored turret, although ammunition racks are visible. Note also the somewhat precariously secured M136 rocket next to the gunner's position. (Courtesy US Air Force, photo by Senior Airman Ali E. Flisek)

Group (NSWDG), Gray Fox, and the Rangers. The JSOTF was responsible for hunting down al-Qaeda bombmakers, leaders, and logistics cells along with nationalist Sunni and Shia insurgents. General David Petraeus, theater commander in Iraq, was quoted as saying that 22 SAS (and the JSOTF) "… have helped immensely in the Baghdad area, in particular, to take down the al-Qaeda car bomb networks and other al-Qaeda operations in Iraq's capital city, so they have done a phenomenal job in that regard."

For covert operations requiring either physical mobile surveillance or a low-profile approach to a target location, the SF soldiers use a mix of commercial vehicles ranging from well-worn, locally purchased Toyota Corollas and Volkswagen Minibuses, to older Mercedes and BMWs along with some armored and unarmored SUVs. All are fitted with local Iraqi license plates and feature local stickers and accruements to appear to any interested observers as nothing out of the ordinary. Task Force operators also often grow Iraqi-style moustaches and dress in full Arab *dishdasha* or *thawb* to blend in, with reports of UKSF personnel even using makeup products to darken their skins.

When the operation is considered overt, such as a deliberate action raid against an al-Qaeda safe house with UAV and helicopter gunship support, the operators drive to the target in their Pandur AGMS or hitch a ride with Stryker- or Bradley-equipped mechanized units. Some 22 SAS elements operating with Task Force Black in Baghdad used borrowed M1114 up-armored HMMWVs and GMVs as they operated closely alongside Delta before these vehicles were replaced with the Bushmaster, as detailed later. UKSF operating with the Maneuver or Strike Battlegroup in southeastern Iraq followed a similar pattern, with the SF element often protected by a strike group of a pair of

An excellent view of the rear bed of the current ECV GMV-S SF version. This vehicle was deployed in Iraq and both centerline and rear weapons stations are clearly shown. Note also the equipment holdall mounted to the back of the driver's seat for easy access to spare magazines, batteries, and other essentials. (Courtesy Rob Skipper)

Challenger II MBTs and a Warrior platoon carrying the battalion's recce platoon, engineer and medical support, and the SF element itself. The recce platoon was also trained to support the SF team in the break-in on the target. The heavy armor would then escort the SF element out after the target was breached and exploited.

THE RISE OF THE MRAP

The first MRAPs appeared in limited numbers in Iraq as EOD and combat engineer vehicles, such as the BAE Land Systems RG-31. Originally designed based on South African and Rhodesian bush war experience, generically MRAPs are based on a V-shaped or curved lower hull that directs the blast from a land mine or IED around and away from the vehicle. Additionally, MRAPs are generally fully enclosed vehicles, belying their origins as EOD vehicles, with windscreens and viewing ports fitted with heavy ballistic glass.

As the IED threat increased in Iraq, MRAPs were seen as the safest answer to a threat that was costing the lives of hundreds of service personnel a year. Although certainly far better protected than HMMWVs or Snatch or WMIK Land Rovers, the early MRAPs were not designed as infantry transports and were often seen as too bulky, too tall, and too heavy for either the urban environments of Iraq or the mountainous regions and poor roads of Afghanistan. New designs are being developed with both the tactical needs of their occupants and the operational environments in mind – although criticism has been voiced of their effect on the COIN effort, as they encourage soldiers to travel in these vehicles rather than on foot interacting with the local population. Additionally, the heavier designs also forced patrols to stick to the roads, thus telegraphing their routes to the insurgents.

There are three major categories of MRAPs in use in Iraq and Afghanistan. Category I (Mine Resistant Utility Vehicles or MRUVs) are lighter-weight patrol vehicles; Category II (Joint Explosive Ordnance Disposal Rapid Response Vehicles or JERRVs) are larger and designed for convoy security, MEDEVAC, EOD, or engineer tasks; Category III are the heavyweight specialist EOD and route-clearance vehicles.

USSOCOM has deployed MRAPs produced by BAE Land Systems – the 9-ton 4x4 RG-31 Pathfinder and the RG-33 in both 4x4 and

The up-armored turret of a GMV-S from an early Frag Kit (Fragmentary Armour Kit) deployed to Iraq mounted with .50 M2. Note the ballistic glass fitted to the lower half of the Objective Gunner Protection Kit (OGPK) shield to allow the gunner to look forward under the gun shield. (Courtesy Rob Skipper)

6x6 configurations as the USSOCOM Armored Utility Vehicle (AUV). The SOF versions of the RG-31 and RG-33 differ in many respects from similar vehicles featuring remote weapons stations (RWSs) deployed by the United States and UK: GMV-style swing-arm weapon mounts; increased seating (from six in a standard RG-31 to eight in the USSOCOM version); an SOF-specific communications suite; Blue Force Tracker; and a thermal driver's sight. They also feature an upgradeable armor kit, allowing units to configure the vehicle to match local threat levels.

UKSF also decided that they required an MRAP Category I vehicle to transport strike teams to urban target locations and the UK Special Forces Group purchased 24 Australian Thales Bushmaster Infantry Mobility Vehicles (IMVs) in mid-2008. These Bushmasters were intended solely for operations in Iraq in support of Task Force Black and the resident SF element operating with British forces in the Basra area. The Bushmasters have received an aftermarket armor package and anti-IED ECM features along with an RWS-mounted M2 heavy machine-gun.

G

1: RG-33 MINE RESISTANT AMBUSH PROTECTED (MRAP), US SPECIAL OPERATIONS COMMAND (USSOCOM) VARIANT: COMBINED JOINT SPECIAL OPERATIONS TASK FORCE – ARABIAN PENINSULA (CJSOTF-AP), IRAQ, 2008

The first MRAP vehicle modified specifically for use by USSOCOM units deployed with CJSOTF-AP, this RG-33 shows several distinctive modifications unique to the Special Forces (SF) version. Foremost is the turret-mounted CROWS II remote weapons station (RWS) with M2 Browning. Other changes are the bewildering array of antennae servicing multiple types of communications and electronic countermeasures (ECM) systems, the hood-mounted satellite communications (SATCOM) antennae, and the driver's thermal camera mounted on the roof.

All SF soldiers utilizing the RG-33, and its cousin the RG-31, must complete a pre-deployment week-long course in driving and manning the vehicle and using its weapon systems and communication suites. The SOCOM version features armor designed to counter the deadly Explosively Formed Penetrator (EFP) type of Improvised Explosive Device (IED) and utilizes a customizable up-armoring package, allowing the vehicle to be configured to local threat types. Although well-liked by operators in Iraq, the vehicle proved too top-heavy for many operational areas in Afghanistan and is being supplemented by the new Oshkosh M-ATV in that theatre.

2: AGF SERVAL SPECIAL OPERATIONS VEHICLE: KOMMANDO-SPEZIALKRÄFTE (KSK), AFGHANISTAN, 2009

Forced to deploy to Afghanistan in 2002 with a number of loaned Ground Mobility Vehicles – Special Forces (GMV-S) from the 3rd Special Forces Group, the KSK immediately began the hunt for a new patrol vehicle, resulting in the purchase of the Aufklärungs- und Gefechtsfahrzeug (AGF) Serval, based on the proven G270 CDI Mercedes-Benz G-Wagen. The vehicle illustrated is a model deployed with the KSK detachment with Regional Command North. This vehicle mounts both forward and rear 7.62x51mm MG3 medium machine-guns (MMGs) on GMV-style swing arms (note the EOTech sights) and a Browning M2 .50 machine-gun in the main turret ring. The vehicle is also protected by smoke-grenade dischargers mounted at each corner. Note the sand channels mounted to the sides, used for extracting the vehicle when stuck in loose sand, and also the fold-down stowage boards at the rear of the vehicle carrying crew equipment, ammunition, and essential supplies.

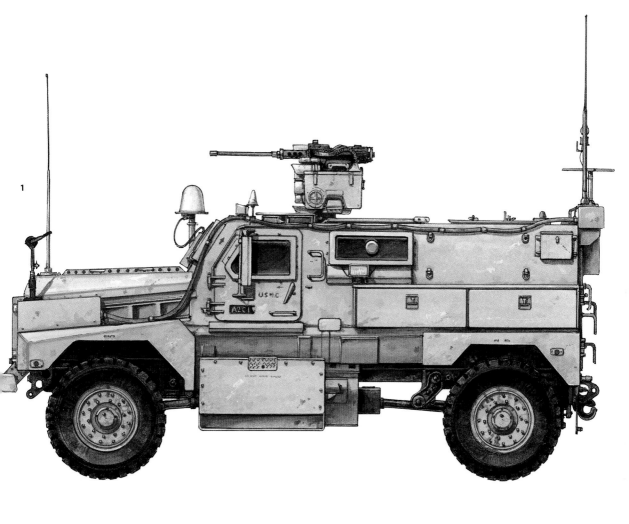

1

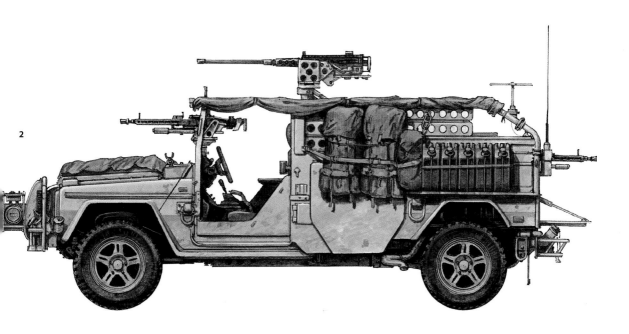

2

A MARSOC MSOB GMV-M in an unusual unit-applied camouflage finish. Note the CREW IED jammer on the right of the hood and self-recovery winch. MARSOC GMVs are often distinguished by the rear side plate up-armor kit, which stretches beyond the tailgate of the vehicle. (Courtesy Rob Skipper)

Although the MRAPs have saved many lives, they do have their drawbacks, particularly for SOF operations. They have a high centre of gravity by design, raising the risk of rollovers, particularly in rural Afghanistan. Additionally, many are too heavy for some of the road and bridge conditions encountered, and the height of the vehicle has caused concern in Iraq because of the potential for accidental electrocution of the crew, as antennae may snag on low-slung power cables.

These concerns have led to the development of a new MRAP, jointly funded by the US Marine Corps and USSOCOM – the MRAP All Terrain Vehicle (M-ATV). The M-ATV is built by Oshkosh Corporation and is a 4x4 vehicle based on the Medium Tactical Vehicle Replacement (MTVR) 7-ton truck equipped with Israeli-designed composite armor. The M-ATV carries four passengers and a gunner in an enclosed armored turret capable of mounting weapons systems ranging from the M240/Mk 48 GPMG to the Mk 19/Mk 47 AGL. It is also perhaps the most high-tech MRAP thus deployed, with its own acoustic sniper detection system and anti-IED ECM as standard features.

Specifically to address the mountainous terrain of Afghanistan, the vehicle features a central tire inflation system with four terrain settings which inflates the tires to cope with difficult ground, plus independent suspension for a smoother ride. It can carry up to 1,800kg of payload. The M-ATV was to enter service with USSOCOM and Marine units in Afghanistan from the end of 2009.

THE FUTURE OF SOF PATROL VEHICLES

As the campaign in Iraq winds down for Coalition forces and perhaps ramps up in what was once known as the "forgotten war" in Afghanistan, what will the future bring for SOF vehicles? The biggest question remaining, and one that perhaps will never be answered to the satisfaction of all, is finding the right balance between protection and mobility. Armor plating, blast-proofing, advanced crew survivability systems, and anti-IED technology all add weight and bulk to a vehicle, not to mention the extra weight of multiple weapons systems and ammunition. Conversely, as discussed earlier, SOF vehicles need to be fast and agile enough in often difficult terrain to be capable of escaping from major contacts with conventional enemy forces.

In addition, the type of vehicle an SOF unit requires

A US Army Special Forces RG-33 with CROWS II RWS mounting the M2 .50 machine-gun. Note the numerous antennae for SATCOM radios and anti-IED ECM systems adorning the MRAP. (Courtesy Tech Sgt Larry W Carpenter Jr., USAF)

for a raid on a remote rural insurgent training camp differs from a similar raid on an urban safe house or bombmaking lab. The rural target may be open to approach from multiple directions, reducing the IED risk, and heavier weapons systems may be needed as the team might have to fight into, and potentially out of, the objective. The urban mission could well face a far higher IED threat and the unit may not require the use of any crew-served weapons, as it quickly conducts a breach then raids the suspect premises, extracting before local insurgent mobs can gather.

An example of the newly deployed Oshkosh M-ATV (right) parked next to an M1113 ECV HMMWV in Afghanistan, showing the minimal differences in height profile compared with other MRAP vehicles. The M-ATV has been specifically developed with the harsh Afghan terrain in mind. (Courtesy Cpl Michael Curvin, US Army)

Both the United States and the UK have pursued somewhat similar strategies in finally providing a range of vehicles for their SOF operators, which collectively may go some way in providing practical answers. Although a costly and logistically difficult exercise, adopting a range of vehicles designed to cater for specific environments and specific threats may be the only way forward for SOF units deployed at the sharp end.

A 19th Special Forces Group HMMWV destroyed by an IED in Afghanistan 2002 – fortunately with only minor injuries to the crew. The vehicle has been stripped of any useful or classified items and awaits recovery or destruction from the air. (Courtesy JZW)

GLOSSARY

4 RAR	4th Battalion, Royal Australian Regiment, now 2 Commando
AGF	Aufklärungs- und Gefechtsfahrzeug
AGMS	Armored Ground Mobility System
AMF	Afghan Militia Forces
ANA	Afghan National Army
ANP	Afghan National Police
APC	armored personnel carrier
ASK	Armor Survivability Kit
ATGM	anti-tank guided missile
ATV	All Terrain Vehicle
AUV	Armored Utility Vehicle
BDA	Bomb Damage Assessment
CJSOTF-AP	Combined Joint Special Operations Task Force – Arabian Peninsula
CJSOTF-N	Combined Joint Special Operations Task Force – North
CJSOTF-W	Combined Joint Special Operations Task Force – West
CROWS	Common Remotely Operated Weapon Station
CSAR	Combat Search and Rescue
DA	direct action
DAP	Direct Action Penetrator
DEVGRU	Naval Special Warfare Development Group
DMVS	Desert Mobility Vehicle System
DMV	Desert Mobility Vehicle
DPV	Desert Patrol Vehicle
E-WMIK	Enhanced Weapon Mount Installation Kit
ECM	electronic countermeasures
ECV	M1113 Enhanced Capacity Vehicle
EFP	Explosively Formed Penetrator
EOD	Explosive Ordnance Disposal
FOB	Forward Operating Base
GMG	Grenade Machine Gun
GMV	Ground Mobility Vehicle
GMV-M	GMV MARSOC variant
GMV-N	GMV Navy variant
GMV-S	GMV – Special Forces
GMV-ST	GMV – Special Tactics
HArD	HMMWV Armored Demountable Kit
HIMARS	High-Mobility Artillery Rocket System
HMMWV	High-Mobility Multi-Purpose Wheeled Vehicle; "Humvee"
HMT	High Mobility Transporter
HSUV	Hardened Sports Utility Vehicle
HVT	high-value target
ICV	Infantry Carrier Vehicle
IED	Improvised Explosive Device
IFAV	Interim Fast Attack Vehicle
IFF	Identification Friend or Foe
IFOR	Implementation Force
IMV	Infantry Mobility Vehicle
IR	infrared
ISAF	International Security Assistance Force
JERRV	Joint Explosive Ordnance Disposal Rapid Response Vehicle
JIEDDO	Joint IED Defeat Organization
JSOC	Joint Special Operations Command
JSOTF	Joint Special Operations Task Force
JTF-2	Joint Task Force-2
KSK	Kommando-Spezialkräfte
LMTV	Light Medium Tactical Vehicles
LRDG	Long Range Desert Group
LRPV	Long Range Patrol Vehicle
LSV	Light Strike Vehicle
M-ATV	MRAP All Terrain Vehicle
M-WMIK	Mobility Weapon-Mounted Installation Kit
MARSOC	Marine Special Operations Command
MEDEVAC	medical evacuation
MOUT	Military Operations in Urban Terrain
MPV	Mine Protected Vehicle
MRAP	Mine Resistant Ambush Protected
MRUV	Mine Resistant Utility Vehicle
MSG	Military Systems Group
MSOB	Marine Special Operations Battalion
MTVR	Medium Tactical Vehicle Replacement
NORSOF	Norwegian Special Operations Forces
NSTV	Non-Standard Tactical Vehicle (or NTV)
NSWDG	Naval Special Warfare Development Group
NZ SAS	New Zealand Special Air Service Group
OAV	Offensive Action Vehicle
ODA	Operational Detachment Alpha
ODB	Operational Detachment Bravo
OEF	Operation *Enduring Freedom* – Afghanistan
OGPK	Objective Gunner Protection Kit
OIF	Operation *Iraqi Freedom*
PB	Patrol Bases
PMV	Protected Mobility Vehicle
QRF	Quick Reaction Force
RSOV	Ranger Special Operations Vehicle
RTF	Reconstruction Task Force
RWS	remote weapons station
SAS	Special Air Service
SASR	Special Air Service Regimemt (Australian Army)
SATCOM	satellite communications
SBS	Special Boat Service
SEAL	Sea, Air and Land teams
SEK	Survival Enhancement Kit
SF	Special Forces
SFOD-D	1st Special Forces Operational Detachment – Delta
SFOR	Stabilization Force
SFTG	Australian Special Forces Task Group
SINGARS	Single-Channel Ground–Air Radio System
SMU	Special Mission Unit
SOAR	Special Operations Aviation Regiment
SOCOMD	Australian Army Special Operations Command
SOF	Special Operations Forces
SOG	Special Operations Group
SOTG	Special Operations Task Group
SOV	Special Operations Vehicle
SR	special reconnaissance
SRV	Surveillance and Reconnaissance Vehicle
SSE	Sensitive Site Exploitations
ST	Special Tactics
STS	Special Tactics Squadron
UKSF	UK Special Forces
USSOCOM	US Special Operations Command
VBIED	vehicle-borne IED
VOSS	Vehicle Optics Sensor System
WMIK	Weapons Mount Installation Kit

INDEX